EMOTIONAL INTELLIGENCE

The Genius Guide To Maximizing Your Emotional Intelligence

DANIEL ROBBINS

Contents

Understanding Intelligence

Nature of Intelligence

Intelligence is a commonly-used word; nonetheless, it does not entail that people have a thorough understanding of what the word really means. A conceptual definition of intelligence is the ability to learn from experience, solve problems and use knowledge to adapt in a specific environment. This definition is said to be applicable across cultures. Indeed, individuals differ in their ability to understand complex ideas to successfully adapt in a particular environment or to overcome obstacles. The differences are undeniable and most of the time they are taken into consideration when it comes to attempts in understanding the concept of intelligence holistically. Individual differences are substantial yet inconsistent at times. How a person responds "intellectually" will differ on varying circumstances and in different realms, as they can be observed and judged according to different criteria.

Up until now, there are still unanswered questions surrounding the concept of intelligence. Several conceptualizations and attempts to map out the entirety of intelligence have surfaced through time yet none command a universal acquiescence. Despite the existence of gray areas, still it can be said that there exists a considerable amount of clarity achieved by years and years of studies and researches in some areas.

INTELLIGENCE: Ability or Abilities?

Charles Spearman (1863-1945) pioneered the notion of *general intelligence*. This *general intelligence*, as Spearman theorized, is linked to several clusters that can be analyzed by using factor analysis. The studies conducted by Spearman revealed that regardless of the domain of a mental test, the scores tend to load on one major factor, a common pool of mental energy, which he labeled as the *g* or the general factor (Neisser, 1996).

The idea of having a single scale of general intelligence was directly opposed by several other psychologists who stand by the notion of multiple mental abilities. L.L. Thurstone, for instance, identified seven clusters of primary mental abilities, which includes the following: inductive reasoning, memory, numerical ability, perceptual speed, spatial ability, verbal comprehension and word fluency. Some contemporary psychologists agreed with this idea of multiple forms of intelligence. Howard Gardner, in his book Frames of Mind (1983), identified eight types of intelligences including: bodily-kinesthetic, intrapersonal, interpersonal, linguistic, logical-mathematical, musical, naturalistic and spatial. Gardner pointed out that the conception of intelligence must not be limited to studies and works with "normal" people. By looking at different cases of people who are "special" or gifted, people who suffered selective brain damage, people with abilities valued by their own culture and the like, Gardner was able to widen the horizon of his understanding and conceptual-ization of intelligence. He even carried the speculation of a ninth form of intelligence he named *existential*, which he described as the ability to think about existence, life and death (Neisser, 1996).

Robert Sternberg is another contemporary theorist, who agreed with Gardner with his conception of multiple intelligences. However, Sternberg proposes only three fundamental aspects of intelligence, which includes analytic, creative and practical. Analytic intelligence pertains to one's ability to acquire and store information. This intelligence is what a typical intelligence test is measuring. Creative intelligence, as characterized by Stern-berg, is the person's ability to think originally. This intelli-gence talks about the person's ability to adapt to novel situations (Neisser, 1996).

THE CHANGING FACE of the Intelligent

The significance of understanding intelligence is incon-testable. For many years, psychologists have been trying to understand, categorize and define human intelligence. Studies and researches have been made to fathom the nature of intelligence and most of the time these works measure intelligence using IQ.

Psychologists recognized, since the eighteenth century, that the mind consists of a three-part division. These parts include cognitive, effect and the motivation (or cognition). The cognitive part is the one responsible for memory, reasoning, abstract thought and judgment. For several years psychologists and other experts usually use the word intelligence to characterize how well this cognitive part of the mind functions (Mayer, 1997).

There are several theories, whether they are hoary or

contemporary, that are elucidating the idea of having more than one aspect or type of intelligence and this has been recognized in the field of psychology for many years. Nevertheless, a good measure of one's cognitive ability suffices the broad notion of intelligence for the past years. Indeed, cognitive intelligence is the kind of intelligence most people know and understand.

This traditional view of intelligence has been challenged and is still being challenged at present. The emerging idea, especially in the contemporary, of broadening the understanding of intelligence paved way to the changing face of who and what can be considered intelligent.

Measuring intelligence using only the cognitive part of the human mind is now seen to be insufficient to understand the full potential of human intelligence. High scores in tests measuring memory, reasoning and logic, mathematical skills, and the like are no longer the best indicators of actual performances.

The New Face of Intelligence

Emotional Intelligence: What Really Is It?

Another form of intelligence, called emotional intelligence, is now gaining considerable attention in various journals, books and magazines. Studies and researches about this intelligence are now continuously growing in numbers. Emotional intelligence, just like any other types of intelligence, is not easy to define. Although there are several authors talking about emotional intelligence, particularly nowadays, there is still no universal definition existing until now.

A broad definition of emotional intelligence states that it is the one responsible for personal, emotional, survival and social dimensions of intelligence. These functions are said to be more important than cognitive aspects of intelligence in day-to-day functioning. Moreover, emotional intelligence is associated with understanding oneself and others, adapting to the immediate surroundings and relating to others to successfully address the demands of the environment.

Emotional intelligence is not really a recent discovery.

It has been known in the field for a relatively long time. It is just now that people began to recognize the big role it plays in the entirety of human intelligence.

In 1940, David Wechsler pioneered the study about emotional intelligence. He called it the "non intellective aspect of general intelligence." According to Wechsler, non intellective factors, which include affect and conative abilities, are not just admissible but are necessary factors of general intelligence. Hence, to fully understand or measure total intelligence, one must assess non intellective factors as well (Grayson).

Following Wechsler's proposition, Leeper, in 1948, stated that "emotional thought" is part of logical thought and intelligence in general. These early recognitions of the importance of emotional intelligence have been succeeded by psychologists of the contemporary milieu. Howard Gardner's theory of multiple intelligences, for instance, included emotional or personal dimension in the form of interpersonal and intrapersonal skills. Other psychologists like Peter Salovey and John Mayer devoted their research to understanding the emotional aspect of intelligence. Their works are concentrating on six components of emotional intelligence, which include the following: assertiveness, empathy, emotional self-awareness, interpersonal relationship, impulse control and stress tolerance (Grayson).

There is a plethora of definitions offered to explain what emotional intelligence is. With the absence of a generic conceptualization, one must start with exploring and understanding the relationship of the two big terms, *emotion* and *intelligence*, to come up with a relatively enlightened idea of what emotional intelligence really is. Emotional intelligence, therefore, can best be described by the following words: "the ability to perceive emotions, to access and generate emotions so as to assist thought, to understand emotions and emotional knowledge and to reflectively regulate emotions so as to promote emotional and intellectual growth" (Mayer, 1997).

The definition provided above is among the best descriptions appropriated for the concept of emotional intelligence. What made it more appealing than others is its encompassing conceptualization of how emotion and intelligence are related. The definition was able to intertwine the notions that one thinks intelligently about emotions and emotions make thinking more intelligent.

As mentioned earlier, emotional intelligence is deemed more necessary in the everyday experience than the cognitive aspect of intelligence. For instance, reasoning that takes emotions into consideration (which is a part of emotional intelligence) is usually present in a person's everyday life. Dealing with other people or socializing and self-awareness are common grounds identifying how well one can manage his/her everyday experience. Responding in a specific situation by assessing social factors and one's emotional knowledge identifies how one would manage surviving his/her immediate environment. All of these factors are aspects of emotional intelligence and these are the reasons why more attention has now been given to studying emotional intelligence as a key factor in determining a person's ability to be successful in life.

Indeed, more and more studies show support that emotional intelligence can be a more accurate indicator of a person's behavior and performance. This aspect of intelligence can help predict success primarily because it reflects how a person would utilize knowledge to his/her immediate situation. Getting along with the world is a key factor for one to be successful in life, and that is exactly what emotional intelligence of a person could identify.

With these reasons some industries are now giving more priority to emotional intelligence than the traditional cognitive aspect.

THE SIGNIFICANCE of Emotional Intelligence

For several years, human intelligence was measured using the IQ yard stick. How well one scores in verbal IQ tests (information comprehension, vocabulary, similarities, digit span and the like) and performance IQ tests (object assembly, digit symbol, picture completion, picture arrangement, block design), was generally used to predict one's success and failure odds. Nevertheless, with the growing numbers of research showing that there is more to intelligence than what cognitive abilities could offer; more and more companies and establishments are now considering looking at a better yardstick to assess intelligence among people, that is, emotional intelligence.

THE INTELLIGENCE of a Social Being

People are social beings. Building relationships with other people is basic to human nature. One cannot just live without forming any kind of connection with the rest of the world. This reality explains why emotional intelligence is important. Emotions have the power to override thoughts and to profoundly influence a person's behavior. Therefore knowing and understanding emotions of the self and others can greatly contribute to building a good and healthy relationship with the rest of the world.

The success in life can be largely attributed to how one handles webbed relationships in certain circumstances. How a person responds to dire situations, for instance, cannot be better explained by how good he/she is in written tests in logic, math or vocabulary than by how he/she developed his/her emotional intelligence.

REDEFINING THE "SMART"

Neither having outstanding scholastic achievements nor having memorized every step in the technical know-how by heart and by experience will no longer guarantee a person his/her dream job. With substantial amount of studies valuing the importance of emotional intelligence to job performances, more and more companies are now utilizing EQ tests to applicants in addition to the traditional IQ tests. Some companies are even giving more priority to EQ results than the IQ scores.

The workplace can be the best ground to see how emotional intelligence redefines what it means to be smart. There are just several intertwining relationships that occur in a workplace. A person needs to deal with several others primarily because they are working as one unit. In such situations, being the most cognitively intelligent individual is one thing, but knowing how to effectively deal with people from different walks of life is surely another thing.

The success of a company relies largely on how well-established are the relationships of the working individuals within the firm. This is the reason why most companies are now looking at the emotional aspect of intelligence of applicants and employees in deciding whom to hire or whom to keep and whom to let go. According to studies, EQ predicts higher performance three times better than IQ. Even leadership requires a higher level of emotional intelligence than of the cognitive one. Thus, it is said that the higher the job position, the more emotional intelligence is needed (Goleman, 1998).

Emotional intelligence, however, must not be mistaken

as just "being nice." Moreover it does not entail completely surrendering to one's feelings. Emotional intelligence determines a person's potential in learning practical skills that are based on elements that include self-regulation, self-awareness, motivation, empathy and adeptness. These skills, unlike the ones measured by IQ, are said to be uncontrolled by genetics and not learned in traditional academe. Everyone can develop the above-mentioned skills.

The New Face of Intelligence

Components of Emotional Intelligence

To fully grasp what emotional intelligence is, identifying its components would be of great help. However, as much as it is difficult to give a definition with universal assent to the concept of emotional intelligence, listing down specific components is posting a certain difficulty as well. There are just plenty of identified components and the list varies as the name of the author responsible for it varies.

The focus of this book will just revolve around some components that are commonly shared by different conceptualizations of the contemporary. This includes the following: self-awareness, self-regulation, empathy, interpersonal relationship, social responsibility and stress management.

Self-awareness includes emotional awareness or the ability to recognize that emotions influence performances. Moreover it holds the ability to use values as a guiding light in decision making processes. Self-awareness also includes realistic and accurate self-assessment. This is the ability to identify one's strengths and weaknesses and the capability to learn from experience.

Self-regulation talks about the ability to control oneself in the sense of effectively managing disruptive impulses and emotions. Also this skill involves adaptability or the ability to flexibly handle challenges and changes.

Empathy involves understanding feelings and perspectives of other people. Moreover an empathetic individual takes active interest in others' concerns, is service oriented, and is politically, socially and culturally aware.

Interpersonal relationships skill is the ability to create and keep a mutually satisfying relationship characterized by giving and receiving functions and intimacy. This skill involves being able to maintain meaningful social interactions that are rewarding and enjoyable.

Social responsibility is an emotional intelligence component that includes the ability to act responsibly as a member of a society, even if there are no personal merits gained in the process. This skill demonstrates a person's recognition that he/she is an element of a larger world; thus, being cooperative and contributing are seen to be essential.

Stress management involves stress tolerance, which is the ability to withstand stressful events or adverse situations without getting too overwhelmed. Dealing with stress, perhaps, is one of the most common problems experienced by several individuals; thus, a portion of this book will provide more information about the said problem. How well people manage stress can be helped by well-developed emotional intelligence through stress tolerance skill.

Stressing Stress

The more complicated life gets, the higher the stress rates seem to be. In today's fast-paced environment, stressors seem to multiply for every hour that passes by. Stress is a common problem encountered by people at work, in school and even at home. Although the effects of stress are more noticeable nowadays, the term is actually not a new one. To denote hardship and anxiety, the word stress was used as early as the 14th century (Lubusclen, 1981).

Stress is a mental, physical and emotional response to perceived threats. Contrary to what most people think about stress as entirely rooting from negative experiences, positive events can cause stress too. Moreover, stress can actually be healthy for a person. It focuses individuals on critical needs aside from motivating learning. Nonetheless, there are forms of stress that are pathological and can later on develop as a symptom of a psychological disorder. Also, there are several negative effects on the physical and mental health of a person exposed to prolonged stress (Kant & Sharma, 2012).

According to Brown and Kelly (1979), a stressful event

happens when a person suddenly developed the feeling of helplessness or loss of control over whatever the event is bringing coupled with loss of social and emotional support system. Also, there appears to be some anticipation of physical or emotional pain and the person's active avoidance of the event, which is perceived as unpleasant.

Stress can be a common experience to people all over the world. Generally speaking, stress can come from different sources. Life events whether customary or unexpected can be sources of stress. Relationships can also be a breeding ground for varying forms of stress. Almost every aspect of human life could possibly turn into a particular source of stress and among the most common areas include the workplace.

HOW TO HANDLE Stress

Several studies show that emotional intelligence alleviates the effects of stress. Emotional intelligence is the capacity to reason with emotion. With emotional intelligence, a person is able to perceive his/her emotions as well as others'. Moreover a person can incorporate his/her perceived emotion to thoughts as he/she can understand and effectively manage these emotions. Therefore, having a well-developed emotional intelligence will allow one to withstand any stressors he/she might encounter in life.

As discussed earlier, stress can be anywhere. It can be found in the different areas of a person's life. Stress seems to be ever-present primarily because the person is the one carrying it. Stress is a reaction, a response coming from a person who feels stranded to specific stimulus perceived to be unpleasant.

Dealing with stress does not need any medical prescription unless the person involved has an underlying condition such as depression or some form of anxiety disorder. Self-help and self-management techniques are the usual methods used by people suffering from stress.

Proven to have various health and mental benefits, exercise is one of the most effective ways to combat stress. Breathing techniques can also reduce the pressure that stress is causing the mental and even physical well-being of a person. Moreover other relaxation techniques like yoga and meditation are gathering a considerable amount of attention nowadays from people experiencing trouble with stress.

Nothing beats having a healthy diet in preventing health issues including stress. Reducing the amount of coffee intake and other beverages containing caffeine can also help mediate the effects of stress to the body.

Finally, talking to family, friends and colleagues will greatly help reduce the burden a person is carrying. Seeking some professional help is recommended if stress is experienced for a prolonged period of time affecting several facets of a person's life.

Stress can be caused by several different factors; thus the best remedy can be provided once the source of stress is identified.

Emotionally Self- Aware

Self-awareness: How to Develop It

It all starts from within. Knowing and understanding one's self is the basic step to understand the rest of the world. This explains why the component of emotional intelligence called self-awareness plays a pivotal role.

Self-awareness is the ability to understand one's emotions. The first stage to self-awareness is being conscious of the emotions felt. Sometimes people get confused with what they feel primarily because of the confluence of factors and emotions themselves. A person who will be joining a contest can say that he is excited and scared at the same time.

The second stage involves knowing what triggers the emotion felt. Sometimes people get mad for reasons that they cannot specify. A certain event would always include several stimulus thus one must be able to pinpoint which causes the emotion felt. This stage is important for this is the key for one to be able to control the sudden surfacing of negative feelings.

The third stage is all about understanding how one's

emotion affects him/her as well as other people. Most of the time people are not fully mindful of how their feelings influence their own selves. For instance, people who tend to dwell on the negativities of their lives will suffer not just poor emotional health but also poor physical health.

Understanding these stages is a leap towards developing self-awareness. To further the experience, one can ask some help from people he/she trusts the most to help in observing emotional and behavioral patterns. This is because developing self-awareness is difficult to accomplish successfully if a person will only use his/her perspective. A person will never know the things he never knew about him/herself, unless someone will tell him/her.

Having a journal will also help develop self-awareness. People cannot just commit everything to memory. Writing down whatever happened in an event, how one felt about it and what triggered the feeling as soon as possible will give more accurate details later on during review than with just recalling it by memory. This will largely contribute to seeing patterns and of course in creating solutions for any unwanted behavior steered by strong urges of emotions.

Self-awareness includes one's acceptance of the responsibilities over any actions done. Thus, identifying all the possible outcomes of the noted emotional responses would be a good way to consciously encourage adjustments if necessary.

Being observant is what's important when it comes to developing self-awareness. One must be honest and accurate with the details of what was observed regardless if it is saying a good thing or a bad thing about him/her. Being aware is the beginning of change.

Unspoken Words

Understanding Non-Verbal Communications

People who have been focusing their studies on individual differences represented the groundwork for emotional intelligence. Similar to emotional intelligence, non-verbal skills are significant for success in different aspects of human life. Studies reveal that non-verbal abilities and skills are pivotal in beginning and sustaining social interaction, handling impressions and developing interpersonal relationships. Non-verbal skills are also linked with career success in different business settings and even with stress management (Riggio, 1996).

Verbal communication is considered as a primary means of communication with other people; nonetheless, only a fraction of the messages people send and receive can be accounted to verbal exchanges. Studies suggest that as much as 70-90% of the entire spectrum of communication is nonverbal. Indeed, most of the time the most important messages are encoded in the non-verbal cues of a person. In communicating with other people, therefore, one must pay attention not just to the words uttered but also to the things left unsaid.

Aside from carrying most of the messages, non-verbal communication is what people believe in when it happens that the verbal and nonverbal communications are incongruent.

Compared with verbal exchanges, non-verbal communication is more difficult to fully comprehend for there are factors that must be considered before decoding a gesture. An example is the relativity of non-verbal cues. Cultural differences play an important role in nonverbal communication. There are several gestures that carry different meanings across cultures. An acceptable gesture in one culture might be offensive in the other. In addition to this, a single gesture can mean two or three different things.

IMPORTANT NON-VERBAL CUES

Space, hand and arms, and feet are some of the most common non-verbal information carriers.

Taking up space sends the message of dominance. Women tend to take up lesser space by sitting with legs crossed, sitting tucked under the table and by even stacking materials neatly on desks. Men, on the other hand, sit with feet on floor, arms spread out on a table or on side of chairs and sits pushed back from the table.

If there is a body part that gives accurate cues, it would be the hands provided that there are more nerves connecting the brain and hands than the other parts of the body. If a person holds his/her own hands, it can be associated with feeling anxious or with restraint. Hands closed with palms facing down show being unreceptive and authoritative while hands open with palms up reflect honesty and receptiveness. Hands hiding at the back or in pockets are showing disagreement or unwillingness to converse.

Partial crossing of arms shows that the person is trying to soothe himself/herself and the act is associated with low self-esteem and anxiety. Crossed arms reflect a closed attitude like defiance, resistance or withdrawal.

People do not usually control their legs or feet for they are not conscious about them; thus, feet or legs can give accurate messages about attitudes and feelings. Often, feet or legs point into the direction the person wanted to go or to something the person is interested in. An open stance indicates confidence while standing with closed legs or feet shows anxiety.

These are just some of the many nonverbal cues that are worth noting when communicating with people. The good news about non-verbal communication is that it can be a skill that people develop through time.

A Cup of Laughter

Bringing Humor and Playfulness in Life

Laughter is indeed the best medicine; cliché and true. Adding humor and laughter to one's life does not just bring enjoyment and giggles; it has been proven by countless researches that they are promoting good health as well. Among the health benefits of laughter and humor are enhancing the immune system, reducing stress, muscle tension and anxiety, increasing pain tolerance, improving food digestion and reducing blood pressure.

In today's life most people tend to forget the impor- tance of laughter, humor and playfulness in the everyday experience. Some get too serious about their jobs and responsibilities in life that they tend to reduce their time for themselves to nothing at all. Indeed life is busy especially nowadays, but one cannot be too busy to have even a cup of laughter a day.

There are just several ways on how to introduce and reintroduce humor and laughter to one's life. The following are simple yet effective ways that one could try out:

- Reading funny novels, books and comics. The humor section of bookstores, libraries and DVD rentals will definitely have something that matches a person's sense of humor.

- Creating a "Get your laughter here" corner. One can transform a specific area on the wall at home or in the office for his/her favorite jokes of all time or funny movie lines or even funny pictures to be posted. Sharing these to other people is a better idea. One can allow friends and co-workers to post the funniest joke they've ever heard and the like.

-Watching comedies on television or by visiting comedy bars can bring back one's "laughing-out-loud" with friends.

-Surrounding one's self with positive social ambiance. Joining a crowd who loves sharing jokes and funny experiences is healthy for a person. People tend to laugh more when in a group than when they are alone; thus sharing laughter with others will multiply the positive health effects of humor to one's health.

These are just some of the many ways on how one can enjoy laughter and humor while taking advantage of the health benefits they offer.

ADDING Some Hue of Playfulness

Aside from humor, playfulness is an important ingredient that makes life worth living. Playing is not just for kids. A person who includes playfulness in his/her everyday life is giving a new vibrant hue in his/her seemingly plainly colored world. Adults usually see things the same way over and over when they stick to their linear and problem-solving oriented mindset. This kind of mindset produces a kind of perspective that is failing to see the world in a different and better point of view.

Kids play a lot; thus, spending time with kids will definitely bring out the playful side of a person. Other ways to get one's feet back on the ground of playfulness are watching silly animal videos, playing with active dogs and doing art without intending to come up with an outstanding piece. Deciding which direction to go using a coin flip can make going out for walk more interesting and playful. Adults always tend to think within the box. Creativity is lessened primarily because as adults, people think according to categories. In playfulness, adults make connections they would not normally create. In the land of play, people forget about the rules and limitations, people embrace spontaneity and people use the parts of their brain that do not care about deadlines.

Emotional intelligence is important to maximize the capabilities of a person and by giving oneself humor, laughter and playfulness, one is developing healthy emotional stability. This will be very useful to effectively adapt to a fast-changing world.

The Kind of Intelligence Needed

Resolving Conflicts Positively

Another good way to enhance emotional intelligence is practicing how to handle conflicts positively. There are several strong emotions involved in a conflict; thus, if one knows and understands emotions, he/she can handle even the most heated conflict to ever occur in his/her life.

Conflicts can be viewed in a positive light. People caught in a conflict will have a chance to know themselves better and at the same time explore other people's perspectives. Nonetheless, the manner of resolving conflicts will greatly influence the relationships of the people after the incident.

Solving conflicts positively requires a person to have a healthy emotional intelligence. Understanding how one feels is pivotal in such circumstances. Anger is the dominating emotion whenever there is conflict. By using effective listening skills, a person can defuse the anger of another person; nonetheless, if the anger of another is directed to the person himself, being objective and definitive will be more challenging. This situation requires strong emotional skills to be handled positively.

To respond accordingly to a conflict, one must first be able to recognize and understand the needs of the angry person. An angry person needs to vent out his negative emotion and one must be able to use his/her communication skill to allow the person to voice out this anger. The person who is letting off steam wanted to get the listener's attention and by using non-verbal communication skills the listener can send in cues that he/she is indeed listening. Finally, an angry person needs to be understood. A person who is really mad is actually seeking for some empathy; he/she needs to feel that the listener understands his/her emotion.

The listener or the receiver of the anger must be able to keep an open mind and an understanding heart to handle the situation accordingly. The listener must have tons of patience to let the angry person finish expressing himself/herself. Sincerity of acknowledgments of feelings and empathy must be present. Most importantly, the listener must be able to stay calm whatever words will be thrown at him/her by the angry person. The person might shout and curse and those are elements the listener cannot have a direct control over. Instead the listener can control how he/she responds to those elements.

Once the anger is defused, both parties can now have a chance to sit down and talk things through. Disagreements can always arise, but two rational beings can come up with agreements along the way.

Resolving conflict positively is not an easy task for people who can easily be moved by outbursts of emotions. One must be able to develop their emotional intelligence to effectively adapt to different circumstances that life might bring.

SECTION II:
Emotional Intelligence

EQ vs. IQ

Introduction

The term "Emotional Intelligence" is beginning to enter mainstream vernacular. It is tossed around, in its abbreviation EQ, or EI, and has taken on a shade that reflects the more intuitive side of the human consciousness. While many casual practitioners and novices may have given term this connotation, its actual meaning and ramifications go deeper and have a greater impact on the individual, the social fabric, and this species, in general.

In our quest to understand the meaning of the term, as well as gain an appreciation of its effect, we need to peel back the rhetoric and dive into the conciseness of the self, as well as the intelligence of the trained mind.

To understand Emotional Intelligence, we need to understand the concept of intelligence and the various branches of it. We can broadly differentiate intelligence into two categories. One being cerebral intelligence, or rather IQ; and the second being the Emotional Intelligence, commonly referred to as EQ.

Until now, EQ has seemed to be the counterbalance to IQ. It is promoted by some as the answer to all the failings one experiences when relying on IQ. However, neither EQ nor IQ are well suited to handle the complexities of life on its own. If however, one were to advance their IQ abilities and their EQ abilities, then the resulting advances in tandem end up feeding off of each other resulting in a higher level of overall intelligence and a better appreciation of life and a more fulfilling experience.

The significance of understanding intelligence is incontestable. For many years, psychologists have been trying to understand, categorize and define human intelligence. Studies and researches have been made to fathom the nature of intelligence and most of the time these works measure intelligence using IQ. Therein lies one of the problems. While science has been trying to quantify intelligence, it has found its methods wanting, and as a result, we have been left with only known quantifiable methods that have resulted in using only observable, measurable and categorizable data. Anything outside this has been left out.

During that time, human intelligence was measured using the IQ yardstick. How well one scores in verbal IQ tests (information comprehension, vocabulary, similarities, digit span and the like) and performance IQ tests (object assembly, digit symbol, picture completion, picture arrangement, block design), was generally used to predict one's success and failure odds. Nevertheless, with the growing numbers of research showing that there is more to intelligence than what cognitive abilities could offer; more and more companies and establishments are now considering looking at a better yardstick to assess intelligence among people, that is, emotional intelligence.

9

Predominance of Halves

While we explore the Intelligence halves, it would be wise of us to also understand that there are at least two broad categories we need to appreciate. The first is that we are creatures with distinct chemical profiles. We are after all made up of natural elements, Carbon, Hydrogen, Oxygen, and so on. Different composition ratios, measured in miniscule amounts, result in different metabolic levels, mood levels and characteristics, which essentially confer upon us our individuality and our character.

THE SECOND IS that we are products of our experience. A human child raised in isolation (this is just a thought exercise) will react very differently to a certain stimuli, than a child that is born and raised by his parents, or a child raised in an orphanage. We are undoubtedly and unmistakably a product of our experiences. Even the way we learn and understand things that are communicated to us will differ from one person to the next.

. . .

WHEN WE UNDERSTAND these two issues, we can begin to appreciate that we need to know where we currently stand before we can plot or seek to travel the road to EI. There are two camps which we can identify and categorize the average human character. From this point of identification, we can then chose to plot a course to total Intelligence, first stopping at the implementation of IQ, then proceeding to the implementation of EI then combining the two to result in total intelligence. Let's classify this as Characteristic P and Characteristic Q. Based on this list, you should be able to arrive at a classification of which side of Intelligence you are dominant.

CHARACTERISTIC P

Prone to anger, anxiety or otherwise easily disheveled
Unable to appreciate the ramifications of their actions
Out of touch with your own feelings
Inward looking
Impulsive

CHARACTERISTIC Q

Always positive
Hardly impetuous
In control of emotions
Expressive
Aware of strengths and weaknesses
Patient
Calm even in the face of stress

ONCE YOU LOOK at these traits, leave that in the back of your mind and figure out which you are. It's a short list, but the genius of this list is not in it being something you check and get a result. It's meant for you to cogitate while you go about reading the next section. You will be surprised to find out which half dominates you when we get to that chapter down the road.

10

Understanding Intelligence

Nature of Intelligence

In our quest to redefine intelligence, we find there are a number of pitfalls we need to avoid to arrive at what could be a proper description of sentience and intelligence. The mind is the nexus between the universe and our consciousness. To look at the mind as merely an organic CPU is highly understating its capability. Instead, one needs to adopt a deeper appreciation of the mind and an understanding that its purpose is not limited to merely regulating activities or planning dinner. The mind, when appreciated holistically, reveals a powerful asset that is often times underestimated.

TO SIMPLIFY MATTERS, let us separate the mind, as if it were a physical object. Let's delineate its functions by imagining its abstract functions into physical dimensions. To do this let us take one part of it as the Cerebral Mind, and the other as the Emotional Mind.

. . .

A CONCEPTUAL DEFINITION of intelligence is the ability to learn from experience, solve problems and use knowledge to adapt in a specific environment. This definition is said to be applicable across cultures. Indeed, individuals differ in their ability to understand complex ideas to successfully adapt in a particular environment or to overcome obstacles. The differences are undeniable and most of the time they are taken into consideration when it comes to attempts in understanding the concept of intelligence holistically. How a person responds "intellectually" will differ on varying circumstances and in different realms, as they can be observed and judged according to different criteria.

ONE OF THE reasons that most people are not able to tap into to the powerful functions of their mind is because they are focusing on just the cerebral intelligence and abandoning their emotional intelligence. The nature of true intelligent, or rather, the nature of the truly intelligent individual is that he or she has mastered the ability to tap into the full resources of using their cerebral intelligence and their emotional intelligence.

DIFFERENTIATING Cerebral from Emotional Intelligence

One way to appreciate CI, is to think about it as one's conscious mind. It is the side of the mind that you use to think things through. It is the part of the mind that occupies your present moment. When you are using it, it's what you are aware of. When you count, calculate, decipher, converse – and you are aware of it, you are using CI.

.   .   .

IN COLLEGE, or wherever else you took a calculus class, you will remember the methodical steps that one progresses step by step on paper, to travel from problem to solution. Sometimes mistakes were made, sometimes you steps were forgotten and most times, you got all the steps right getting you to the correct solution. This is one of the examples of CI. You can consciously move the events of a moment from one state to another. You can take a math problem from the state of being a problem, to being a state of a solution and being aware of each step as you progressed.

ON THE OTHER HAND, EI works in exactly the opposite way. You will not be aware of the steps, but you will arrive at the same solution. Most people "feel" their way into the solution. The problem with feeling your way into the solution, is that it gives room for considerable error, especially for those who cannot differentiate the voice of EI and the voice of impulse. Therein lies the reason for EI usually getting a bad wrap for the failings of those who are unable to differentiate the voices.

TO UNDERSTAND intelligence we must accept that combining the two conceptual halves of CI and EI, give us the full breadth of human ability and potential.

Understanding Intelligence from Conventional Thought

Academia has its nomenclature of explaining Intelligence. Charles Spearman (1863-1945) pioneered the notion of *general intelligence.* This *general intelligence,* as Spearman theorized, is linked to several clusters that can be analyzed by using factor analysis. The studies conducted by Spearman revealed that regardless of the domain of a mental test, the scores tend to load on one major factor, a common pool of mental energy, which he labeled as the *g* or the general factor (Neisser, 1996).

THE IDEA of having a single scale of general intelligence was directly opposed by several other psychologists who stand by the notion of multiple mental abilities. L.L. Thurstone, for instance, identified seven clusters of primary mental abilities, which includes the following: inductive reasoning, memory, numerical ability, perceptual speed, spatial ability, verbal comprehension and word fluency. Some contemporary psychologists agreed with this idea of multiple forms of intelligence.

. . .

HOWARD GARDNER, in his book Frames of Mind (1983), identified eight types of intelligences including: bodily-kinesthetic, intrapersonal, interpersonal, linguistic, logical-mathematical, musical, naturalistic and spatial. Gardner pointed out that the conception of intelligence must not be limited to studies and works with "normal" people. By looking at different cases of people who are "special" or gifted, people who suffered selective brain damage, people with abilities valued by their own culture and the like, Gardner was able to widen the horizon of his under-standing and conceptualization of intelligence. He even carried the speculation of a ninth form of intelligence he named *existential*, which he described as the ability to think about existence, life and death (Neisser, 1996).

ROBERT STERNBERG IS another contemporary theorist, who agreed with Gardner with his conception of multiple intelligences. However, Sternberg proposes only three fundamental aspects of intelligence, which includes analytic, creative and practical. Analytic intelligence pertains to one's ability to acquire and store information. This intelligence is what a typical intelligence test is measuring. Creative intelligence, as characterized by Stern-berg, is the person's ability to think originally. This intelli-gence talks about the person's ability to adapt to novel situations (Neisser, 1996).

UNLIKE OUR EARLIER SIMPLIFICATION, psychologists recognized, since the eighteenth century, that the mind consists of a three-part division. These parts include cognitive, effect and the motivation (or cognition). The cognitive part is the one responsible for memory, reasoning, abstract thought and judgment. For several years psychologists and other experts usually use the word intelligence to characterize how well this cognitive part of the mind functions (Mayer, 1997).

THERE ARE SEVERAL THEORIES, whether they are hoary or contemporary, that are elucidating the idea of having more than one aspect or type of intelligence and this has been recognized in the field of psychology for many years. Nevertheless, a good measure of one's cognitive ability suffices the broad notion of intelligence for the past years. Indeed, cognitive intelligence is the kind of intelligence most people know and understand.

HOWEVER, as time progressed, we began to witness the expansion of views and it became mainstream that the definition of intelligence that was limited to just quantifiable IQ testing and similar parameters, were just not sufficient. This traditional view of intelligence has been challenged and is still being challenged at present. The emerging idea, especially in the contemporary, of broadening the understanding of intelligence paved way to the changing face of who and what can be considered intelligent.

MEASURING intelligence using only the cognitive part of the human mind is now seen to be insufficient to understand the full potential of human intelligence. High scores in tests measuring memory, reasoning and logic, mathematical skills, and the like are no longer the best indicators of actual performances.

The New Face of Intelligence

Emotional Intelligence: What Really Is It?

That brings us to the topic of this book on emotional intelligence, which is now gaining considerable attention in various journals, articles and magazines. Studies and researches about this version of intelligence are now continuously growing and the body of work has reached critical mass. Emotional intelligence however has a significant challenge in its path. Because the body of work that has preceded it in academia is concerned with quantifiable, categorizable and definable concepts, we simply do not have the language and vocabulary to describe and define this version of Intelligence, and thus most attempts at doing so result in sounding like a snake oil salesman's pitch. Defining it has become its greatest challenge. Although there are several authors talking about emotional intelligence, particularly nowadays, there is still no universal definition existing until now.

A broad description of emotional intelligence states that it is responsible for personal survival, adaptation as well as the social dimensions of intelligence. That is essentially on the right track, but ultimately incomplete. These functions are also said to be more important than cognitive aspects of intelligence in day-to-day functioning. Moreover, emotional intelligence is associated with understanding oneself and others, adapting to the immediate surroundings and relating to others to successfully address the demands of the environment.

Emotional intelligence is not really a recent discovery. It has been known in the field for a relatively long time. It is just now that people began to recognize the big role it plays in the entirety of human intelligence.

In 1940, David Wechsler pioneered the study about emotional intelligence. He called it the "non intellectual aspect of general intelligence." According to Wechsler, non intellectual factors, which include affect and cognitive abilities, are not just admissible but are necessary factors of general intelligence. Hence, to fully understand or measure total intelligence, one must assess non intellectual factors as well (Grayson).

Following Wechsler's proposition, Leeper, in 1948, stated that "emotional thought" is part of logical thought and intelligence in general. These early recognitions of the importance of emotional intelligence have been succeeded by psychologists of the contemporary milieu. Howard Gardner's theory of multiple intelligences, for instance, included emotional or personal dimension in the form of interpersonal and intrapersonal skills. Other psychologists like Peter Salovey and John Mayer devoted their research to understanding the emotional aspect of intelligence. Their works are concentrating on six components of emotional intelligence, which include the following: assertiveness, empathy, emotional self-awareness, interpersonal relationship, impulse control and stress tolerance (Grayson).

There is a plethora of definitions offered to explain what emotional intelligence is. With the absence of a generic conceptualization, one must start with exploring and understanding the relationship of the two big terms, emotion and intelligence, to come up with a relatively enlightened idea of what emotional intelligence really is. Emotional intelligence, therefore, can best be described by the following words: "the ability to perceive emotions, to access and generate emotions so as to assist thought, to understand emotions and emotional knowledge and to reflectively regulate emotions so as to promote emotional and intellectual growth" (Mayer, 1997).

The definition provided above is among the best descriptions appropriated for the concept of emotional intelligence. What made it more appealing than others is its encompassing conceptualization of how emotion and intelligence are related. The definition was able to inter-twine the notions that one thinks intelligently about emotions and emotions make thinking more intelligent.

As mentioned earlier, emotional intelligence is deemed more necessary in the everyday experience than the cognitive aspect of intelligence. For instance, reasoning that takes emotions into consideration (which is a part of emotional intelligence) is usually present in a person's everyday life. Dealing with other people or socializing and self-awareness are common grounds identifying how well one can manage his/her everyday experience. Responding in a specific situation by assessing social factors and one's emotional knowledge identifies how one would manage surviving his/her immediate environment. All of these factors are aspects of emotional intelligence and these are the reasons why more attention has now been given to studying emotional intelligence as a key factor in determining a person's ability to be successful in life.

Indeed, more and more studies show support that emotional intelligence can be a more accurate indicator of a person's behavior and performance. This aspect of intelligence can help predict success primarily because it reflects how a person would utilize knowledge to his/her immediate situation. Getting along with the world is a key factor for one to be successful in life, and that is exactly what emotional intelligence of a person could identify. With these reasons some industries are now giving more priority to emotional intelligence than the traditional cognitive aspect.

Social Creatures

Most of the species are social. We share an ecosystem and thus are brought together by necessity. That necessity grows to economies of scale, which cause us to live in ever increasing proximity. As that proximity increases, our interaction within the community is fostered. All in all there is too many data points that come across our minds for the consciousness to handle single handedly. The prevalence of data points in human interactions, from reading body language, to analyzing best responses is a heavy toll on the consciousness.

SOCIAL INTERACTIONS REQUIRE A MUCH HIGHER processing capacity than what Cerebral Intelligence can muster. This where EI comes in. It is also one of the reasons, those with stronger EI tendencies make better social interactions and are what is called a "people person". To make it as a good communicator, you must be able to read the cues and respond accordingly. One must be able to put a lot of information, or data points, together and interpret the meaning. Cerebral intelligence is not capable of adequately coping. As such, those who are reliant on CI to make it through the day, find themselves overwhelmed in social situations aside from the regular niceties. As time progresses and more mistakes are encountered, those without proper EQ skills start to misunderstand and eventually reduce their reliance on it.

THE INTELLIGENCE of a Social Being

People are social beings. Building relationships with other people is basic to human nature. One cannot just live without forming any kind of connection with the rest of the world. This reality explains why emotional intelligence is important. Emotions have the power to override thoughts and to profoundly influence a person's behavior. Therefore knowing and understanding emotions of the self and others can greatly contribute to building a good and healthy relationship with the rest of the world.

THE SUCCESS in life can be largely attributed to how one handles webbed relationships in certain circumstances. How a person responds to dire situations, for instance, cannot be better explained by how good he/she is in written tests in logic, math or vocabulary than by how he/she developed his/her emotional intelligence.

NEITHER OUTSTANDING SCHOLASTIC achievements nor strong memorization skills will not guarantee a person his/her dream job. With substantial number of studies valuing the importance of emotional intelligence to job performances, more and more companies are now utilizing

EQ tests to applicants in addition to the traditional IQ tests. Some companies are even giving more priority to EQ results than the IQ scores.

THE WORKPLACE CAN BE the best ground to see how emotional intelligence redefines what it means to be smart. There are just several intertwining relationships that occur in a workplace. A person needs to deal with several others primarily because they are working as one unit. In such situations, being the most cognitively intelligent individual is one thing, but knowing how to effectively deal with people from different walks of life is surely another thing.

THE SUCCESS of a company relies largely on how well established are the relationships of the working individuals within the firm. This is the reason why most companies are now looking at the emotional aspect of intelligence of applicants and employees in deciding whom to hire or whom to keep and whom to let go. According to studies, EQ predicts higher performance three times better than IQ. Even leadership requires a higher level of emotional intelligence than of the cognitive one. Thus, it is said that the higher the job position, the more emotional intelligence is needed (Goleman, 1998).

EMOTIONAL INTELLIGENCE, however, must not be mistaken as just "being nice." Moreover it does not entail completely surrendering to one's feelings. Emotional intelligence determines a person's potential in learning practical skills that are based on elements that include self-regulation, self-awareness, motivation, empathy and adeptness. These skills, unlike the ones measured by IQ, are said to be uncontrolled by genetics and not learned in traditional academe. Everyone can develop the above-mentioned skills.

COMPONENTS OF EMOTIONAL *Intelligence*

To fully grasp what emotional intelligence is, identifying its components would be of great help. However, as much as it is difficult to give a definition with universal assent to the concept of emotional intelligence, listing down specific components is posting a certain difficulty as well. There are just plenty of identified components and the list varies as the name of the author responsible for it varies.

The focus of this book will just revolve around some components that are commonly shared by different conceptualizations of the contemporary. This includes the following: self-awareness, self-regulation, empathy, interpersonal relationship, social responsibility and stress management.

Self-awareness includes emotional awareness or the ability to recognize that emotions influence performances. Moreover it holds the ability to use values as a guiding light in decision-making processes. Self-awareness also includes realistic and accurate self-assessment. This is the ability to identify one's strengths and weaknesses and the capability to learn from experience.

SELF-REGULATION TALKS about the ability to control oneself in the sense of effectively managing disruptive impulses and emotions. Also this skill involves adaptability or the ability to flexibly handle challenges and changes.

. . .

EMPATHY INVOLVES UNDERSTANDING feelings and perspectives of other people. Moreover an empathetic individual takes active interest in others' concerns, is service oriented, and is politically, socially and culturally aware.

INTERPERSONAL RELATIONSHIPS SKILL is the ability to create and keep a mutually satisfying relationship characterized by giving and receiving functions and intimacy. This skill involves being able to maintain meaningful social interactions that are rewarding and enjoyable.

SOCIAL RESPONSIBILITY IS an emotional intelligence component that includes the ability to act responsibly as a member of a society, even if there are no personal merits gained in the process. This skill demonstrates a person's recognition that he/she is an element of a larger world; thus, being cooperative and contributing are seen to be essential.

STRESS MANAGEMENT INVOLVES STRESS TOLERANCE, which is the ability to withstand stressful events or adverse situations without getting too overwhelmed. Dealing with stress, perhaps, is one of the most common problems experienced by several individuals; thus, a portion of this book will provide more information about the said problem. How well people manage stress can be helped by well-developed emotional intelligence through stress tolerance skill.

. . .

STRESSING Stress

AS THE WEB of social interaction increases and gets highly sophisticated it seems to complicate life; and a high-stressed life ensues. In today's fast-paced environment, stressors seem to multiply exponentially as one generation gives way to the next. Stress is a common problem at work, in school and even at home. Although the effects of stress are more noticeable nowadays, the term is actually not a new one. To denote hardship and anxiety, the word stress was used as early as the 14th century (Lubusclen, 1981).

STRESS IS THE MENTAL, physical and emotional state experienced during a stream of stimuli. Contrary to what most people think about stress, it does not just occur during periods of negative stimuli, positive events can cause stress too. Stress, in certain forms, can be beneficial to a person. It focuses individuals on critical needs and blurs the unnecessary. Nonetheless, there are forms of stress that are pathological and can later on develop as a symptom of a psychological disorder. Also, there are several negative effects on the physical and mental health of a person exposed to prolonged stress (Kant & Sharma, 2012).

ACCORDING to Brown and Kelly (1979), a stressful event happens when a person suddenly developed the feeling of helplessness or loss of control over whatever the event is bringing coupled with loss of social and emotional support system. Also, there appears to be some anticipation of physical or emotional pain and the person's active avoidance of the event, which is perceived as unpleasant.

. . .

STRESS CAN BE a common experience to people all over the world. Generally speaking, stress can come from different sources. Life events whether customary or unexpected can be sources of stress. Relationships can also be a breeding ground for varying forms of stress. Almost every aspect of human life could possibly turn into a particular source of stress and among the most common areas include the workplace.

THERE IS another way we can look at all this. Imagine, if you will, a whisk and a commercial mixer. If you use small amounts of batter, the whisk can handle the duty and everything is fine. However, if you increase the quantity of batter, the whisk is eventually overloaded and nothing gets done. However, a large quantity of batter can be easily handled in the commercial mixer. Think about your mind in the same way, "You" consciousness, is like the whisk. It can handle a small quantity of stimuli and manage the appropriate response well. However, if you increase the stimuli stream, what you get is an overwhelming feeling and possible breakdown. This is stress, and it does not matter whether the stimuli stream is positive or negative.

WHEN YOU TAKE the abundant stimuli and feed it to the subconscious, then what you get is a situation that is properly matched and no stress results because the subconscious is designed to handle it. Most people have no idea how to do this and land up failing at many of the areas that have many data streams – relationships are such an example.

. . .

HOW TO HANDLE Stress

NOW LET'S look at it from the perspective of EI. Several studies show that emotional intelligence alleviates the effects of stress. Emotional intelligence is the capacity to handle large levels of stimuli and process it without getting overwhelmed. With emotional intelligence, a person is able to perceive his/her emotions as well as others' (large data streams). Moreover a person can incorporate his/her perceived emotion to thoughts as he/she can understand and effectively manage these emotions. Therefore, having a well-developed emotional intelligence will allow one to withstand any stressors he/she might encounter in life.

AS SUCH, there is a second element that seems to be a characteristic that can be found in the different areas of a person's life. Stress seems to be ever-present primarily because the person is the one carrying it. Stress is a reaction, a response coming from a person who feels stranded to specific stimulus perceived to be unpleasant.

DEALING with stress does not need any medical prescription unless the person involved has an underlying condition such as depression or some form of anxiety disorder. Self-help and self-management techniques are the usual methods used by people suffering from stress.

PROVEN TO HAVE various health and mental benefits, exercise is one of the most effective ways to combat stress. Breathing techniques can also reduce the pressure that stress is causing the mental and even physical well-being of a person. Moreover other relaxation techniques like yoga and meditation are gathering a considerable amount of attention nowadays from people experiencing trouble with stress.

NOTHING BEATS HAVING a healthy diet in preventing health issues including stress. Reducing the amount of coffee intake and other beverages containing caffeine can also help mediate the effects of stress to the body.

FINALLY, talking to family, friends and colleagues will greatly help reduce the burden a person is carrying. Seeking some professional help is recommended if stress is experienced for a prolonged period of time affecting several facets of a person's life.

STRESS CAN BE CAUSED by several different factors; thus the best remedy can be provided once the source of stress is identified.

Emotionally Self- Aware

Self-awareness: How to Develop It

It all starts from within. Knowing and understanding one's self is the basic step to understand the rest of the world. This explains why the component of emotional intelligence called self-awareness plays a pivotal role.

SELF-AWARENESS IS the ability to understand one's emotions. The first stage to self-awareness is being conscious of the emotions felt. Sometimes people get confused with what they feel primarily because of the confluence of factors and emotions themselves. A person who will be joining a contest can say that he is excited and scared at the same time.

THE SECOND STAGE involves knowing what triggers the emotion felt. Sometimes people get mad for reasons that they cannot specify. A certain event would always include several stimulus thus one must be able to pinpoint which causes the emotion felt. This stage is important for this is the key for one to be able to control the sudden surfacing of negative feelings.

THE THIRD STAGE is all about understanding how one's emotion affects him/her as well as other people. Most of the time people are not fully mindful of how their feelings influence their own selves. For instance, people who tend to dwell on the negativities of their lives will suffer not just poor emotional health but also poor physical health.

UNDERSTANDING these stages is a leap towards developing self-awareness. To further the experience, one can ask some help from people he/she trusts the most to help in observing emotional and behavioral patterns. This is because developing self-awareness is difficult to accomplish successfully if a person will only use his/her perspective. A person will never know the things he never knew about him/herself, unless someone will tell him/her.

HAVING a journal will also help develop self-awareness. People cannot just commit everything to memory. Writing down whatever happened in an event, how one felt about it and what triggered the feeling as soon as possible will give more accurate details later on during review than with just recalling it by memory. This will largely contribute to seeing patterns and of course in creating solutions for any unwanted behavior steered by strong urges of emotions.

. . .

SELF-AWARENESS INCLUDES one's acceptance of the responsibilities over any actions done. Thus, identifying all the possible outcomes of the noted emotional responses would be a good way to consciously encourage adjustments if necessary.

BEING observant is what's important when it comes to developing self-awareness. One must be honest and accurate with the details of what was observed regardless if it is saying a good thing or a bad thing about him/her. Being aware is the beginning of change.

UNSPOKEN WORDS
Understanding Non-Verbal Communications

PEOPLE WHO HAVE BEEN FOCUSING their studies on individual differences represented the groundwork for emotional intelligence. Similar to emotional intelligence, non-verbal skills are significant for success in different aspects of human life. Studies reveal that non-verbal abilities and skills are pivotal in beginning and sustaining social interaction, handling impressions and developing interpersonal relationships. Non-verbal skills are also linked with career success in different business settings and even with stress management (Riggio, 1996).

VERBAL COMMUNICATION IS CONSIDERED as a primary means of communication with other people; nonetheless, only a fraction of the messages people send and receive can be accounted to verbal exchanges. Studies suggest that as much as 70-90% of the entire spectrum of communication is nonverbal. Indeed, most of the time the most important messages are encoded in the non-verbal cues of a person. In communicating with other people, therefore, one must pay attention not just to the words uttered but also to the things left unsaid.

ASIDE FROM CARRYING MOST of the messages, non-verbal communication is what people believe in when it happens that the verbal and nonverbal communications are incongruent.

COMPARED WITH VERBAL EXCHANGES, non-verbal communication is more difficult to fully comprehend for there are factors that must be considered before decoding a gesture. An example is the relativity of non-verbal cues. Cultural differences play an important role in nonverbal communication. There are several gestures that carry different meanings across cultures. An acceptable gesture in one culture might be offensive in the other. In addition to this, a single gesture can mean two or three different things.

IMPORTANT NON-VERBAL CUES

SPACE, hand and arms, and feet are some of the most common non-verbal information carriers.

. . .

TAKING up space sends the message of dominance. Women tend to take up lesser space by sitting with legs crossed, sitting tucked under the table and by even stacking materials neatly on desks. Men, on the other hand, sit with feet on floor, arms spread out on a table or on side of chairs and sit pushed back from the table.

IF THERE WERE a body part that gives accurate cues, it would be the hands provided that there are more nerves connecting the brain and hands than the other parts of the body. If a person holds his/her own hands, it can be associated with feeling anxious or with restraint. Hands closed with palms facing down show being unreceptive and authoritative while hands open with palms up reflect honesty and receptiveness. Hands hiding at the back or in pockets are showing disagreement or unwillingness to converse.

PARTIAL CROSSING of arms shows that the person is trying to soothe himself/herself and the act is associated with low self-esteem and anxiety. Crossed arms reflect a closed attitude like defiance, resistance or withdrawal.

PEOPLE DO NOT USUALLY CONTROL their legs or feet for they are not conscious about them; thus, feet or legs can give accurate messages about attitudes and feelings. Often, feet or legs point into the direction the person wanted to go or to something the person is interested in. An open stance indicates confidence while standing with closed legs or feet shows anxiety.

. . .

THESE ARE JUST some of the many nonverbal cues that are worth noting when communicating with people. The good news about non-verbal communication is that it can be a skill that people develop through time.

A Cup of Laughter

Bringing Humor and Playfulness in Life

Laughter is indeed the best medicine; cliché and true. Adding humor and laughter to one's life does not just bring enjoyment and giggles; it has been proven by countless researches that they are promoting good health as well. Among the health benefits of laughter and humor are enhancing the immune system, reducing stress, muscle tension and anxiety, increasing pain tolerance, improving food digestion and reducing blood pressure.

In today's life most people tend to forget the importance of laughter, humor and playfulness in the everyday experience. Some get too serious about their jobs and responsibilities in life that they tend to reduce their time for themselves to nothing at all. Indeed life is busy especially nowadays, but one cannot be too busy to have even a cup of laughter a day.

There are just several ways on how to introduce and reintroduce humor and laughter to one's life. The following are simple yet effective ways that one could try out:

- Reading funny novels, books and comics. The humor section of bookstores, libraries and DVD rentals will definitely have something that matches a person's sense of humor.

- Creating a "Get your laughter here" corner. One can transform a specific area on the wall at home or in the office for his/her favorite jokes of all time or funny movie lines or even funny pictures to be posted. Sharing these to other people is a better idea. One can allow friends and co-workers to post the funniest joke they've ever heard and the like.

-Watching comedies on television or by visiting comedy bars can bring back one's "laughing-out-loud" with friends.

-Surrounding one's self with positive social ambiance. Joining a crowd who loves sharing jokes and funny experiences is healthy for a person. People tend to laugh more when in a group than when they are alone; thus sharing laughter with others will multiply the positive health effects of humor to one's health.

These are just some of the many ways on how one can enjoy laughter and humor while taking advantage of the health benefits they offer.

Adding Some Hue of Playfulness

Aside from humor, playfulness is an important ingredient that makes life worth living. Playing is not just for kids. A person who includes playfulness in his/her everyday life is giving a new vibrant hue in his/her seemingly plainly colored world. Adults usually see things the same way over and over when they stick to their linear and problem-solving oriented mindset. This kind of mindset produces a kind of perspective that is failing to see the world in a different and better point of view.

Kids play a lot; thus, spending time with kids will definitely bring out the playful side of a person. Other ways to get one's feet back on the ground of playfulness are watching silly animal videos, playing with active dogs and doing art without intending to come up with an outstanding piece. Deciding which direction to go using a coin flip can make going out for walk more interesting and playful. Adults always tend to think within the box. Creativity is lessened primarily because as adults, people think according to categories. In playfulness, adults make connections they would not normally create. In the land of play, people forget about the rules and limitations, people embrace spontaneity and people use the parts of their brain that do not care about deadlines.

Emotional intelligence is important to maximize the capabilities of a person; and by giving oneself humor, laughter and playfulness, one is developing healthy emotional stability. This will be very useful to effectively adapt to a fast-changing world.

The Kind of Intelligence Needed

Resolving Conflicts Positively

Another good way to enhance emotional intelligence is practicing how to handle conflicts positively. There are several strong emotions involved in a conflict; thus, if one knows and understands emotions, he/she can handle even the most heated conflict to ever occur in his/her life.

CONFLICTS CAN BE VIEWED in a positive light. People caught in a conflict will have a chance to know themselves better and at the same time explore other people's perspectives. Nonetheless, the manner of resolving conflicts will greatly influence the relationships of the people after the incident.

SOLVING conflicts positively requires a person to have a healthy emotional intelligence. Understanding how one feels is pivotal in such circumstances. Anger is the dominating emotion whenever there is conflict. By using effective listening skills, a person can defuse the anger of another person; nonetheless, if the anger of another is directed to the person himself, being objective and definitive will be more challenging. This situation requires strong emotional skills to be handled positively.

TO RESPOND ACCORDINGLY TO A CONFLICT, one must first be able to recognize and understand the needs of the angry person. An angry person needs to vent out his negative emotion and one must be able to use his/her communication skill to allow the person to voice out this anger. The person who is letting off steam wanted to get the listener's attention and by using non-verbal communication skills the listener can send in cues that he/she is indeed listening. Finally, an angry person needs to be understood. A person who is really mad is actually seeking for some empathy; he/she needs to feel that the listener understands his/her emotion.

THE LISTENER or the receiver of the anger must be able to keep an open mind and an understanding heart to handle the situation accordingly. The listener must have tons of patience to let the angry person finish expressing himself/herself. Sincerity of acknowledgments of feelings and empathy must be present. Most importantly, the listener must be able to stay calm with whatever words may be thrown at him/her by the angry person. The person might shout and curse and those are elements the listener cannot have a direct control over. Instead the listener can control how he/she responds to those elements.

. . .

ONCE THE ANGER IS DEFUSED, both parties can now have a chance to sit down and talk things through. Disagreements can always arise, but two rational beings can come up with agreements along the way.

RESOLVING conflict positively is not an easy task for people who can easily be moved by outbursts of emotions. One must be able to develop their emotional intelligence to effectively adapt to different circumstances that life might bring.

17

Power of Reflection

To develop your EI you would have to be on one of two paths. The first is when you are naturally predisposed to being that way. That is when you are genetically and chemically open to using your subconscious mind in processing your data streams. The second is when you are not born that way and instead train yourself to get to that point. This chapter is about training yourself to get to that point.

THE BEST WAY TO get the subconscious working is to use the power of reflection. Reflection is not just the ability to sit down and think about what has happened to you or what you have done. Reflection is a way for you to channel the events that happen to you towards your subconscious, and let it chew on it and get you the right answer.

THE Subconscious

The subconscious is not a location in your brain. It is a dimension. However, it is easier to imagine it like a location and give it coordinates and directions. But therein lies the problem because it creates a misunderstanding of its physical nature. The subconscious coexists with the consciousness of the brain and does so by operating at a different frequency. When the consciousness is dormant, as in during sleep, the subconsciousness remains awake and has more dominance over the body and its actions. Dreaming is in the realm of the subconscious and it can seem real while it is happening. But most time dreams are unintelligible because they are composed and choreographed differently than how the conscious mind usually does things. That's why many of our dreams do not make 'sense'.

HOWEVER, the subconscious has an enormous capacity. Its ability to remember is superior, as its ability to recall. Its ability to process is far ahead anything the consciousness can conjure and its ability to foresee the consequences of an action and compare it to complementary actions or alternative courses of action is superior as well.

THE ONLY PROBLEM is that the output of the subconscious is not easily transmitted between the silence of the subconscious and the chaos of the conscious mind. Many times the right answer to a problem, or the accurate analysis of the situation is not executed simple because the mind has not been able to read the output of the subconscious.

THE ONLY WAY TO transmit the output of the subconscious to the actionable forefront of the mind – the consciousness, is to operate at a specific frequency. Ideally this is done during moments of calm or even during sleep. One of the reasons sleep is very important, is because that is the time the subconscious can 'download' the solutions to the conscious mind. The other way to do it is to willfully reduce the frequency of the mind. That's where reflection and meditation come into place.

FOR THOSE WHO do not have the 'natural' ability to transmit solutions form the subconscious to the conscious, then these moments of reflection are the best way to develop the bridge between the two mental states.

THE MOMENT of reflection is induced by the individual by embracing a lower frequency and stepping back. Before getting into the steps of reaching reflection, it is wise that we remember that the purpose of undertaking this step is to be able to invoke the ability to enhance Emotional Intelligence.

18

The Emotions

To differentiate EI from emotions requires one more step in the process of understanding. First we need to understand that EI is not being emotional. Emotions are different and are triggers that are tied to our instinctual behavior. Emotions are not the same as Emotional Intelligence, and being emotional is not what we are advocating here. They are two, very different things. Being emotional is when you react without the benefit of planning, thought, or understanding of the true matter at hand. EI on the other hand is an understanding of the situation and the calm response to it.

EMOTIONS FORM one of the three axis that determine the action and reaction of a human being. Animals have more instinct and depending on their stage of evolution that instinct can either be aggressive or passive. When those reactions are aggressive, they are usually because the animal is wild. When they are passive, it is because the animal is likely domesticated. In humans, emotions set the stage for a number of issues in one's life. These people are usually impulsive and prone to mistakes. This is the antithesis to EI.

WHICHEVER PERSONALITY one happens to be, it is best to strike a balance between impulsive responses and properly proportioned reactions. The best way to do this is to reflect on a frequent basis. The reflection process creates a personality that is more in tune and connected with the subconscious.

THERE ARE ALSO a number of other areas of the psyche that you need to briefly understand in order to differentiate it and focus on what is necessary. The first is the issue of moods. Moods have a huge impact on our lives and you need to understand it to be able to take advantage of what your subconscious is telling you. Think of moods this way: it is a predisposition. If you are in a bad mood, whatever the stimulus you are faced with, will seem negative. On the other hand, if you are in a good mood, everything you face will feel surmountable.

ON THE OTHER HAND, there is also the issue of 'feelings'. Feelings are like moods, but are distinctly different. Feelings are attributed to an external stimulus while a corresponding emotion is triggered by an internal stimulus. Both are affected by moods.

ONCE YOU HAVE an idea of these, you should be at a point where you realize that there is a lot going on in each of us and most of it is easily digestible, if it is approached with the full resources each of us is endowed with. The problem is that the resource that is best able to handle it operates at a frequency that differs from our conscious reality.

HOW to Properly Reflect

Reflection is not meditation. That's the first hurdle to overcome. Most people tend to confuse the two. Reflection is the process of allowing events to sink in without rushing to judgment or analysis. Reflection is a powerful tool in the quest for invoking and maintaining state of Emotional Intelligence. In the beginning you will only be able to take advantage of the effects of the EI at intervals. As you practice your reflection techniques, the time it takes for the solution to appear in your consciousness decreases and you will find that you are more in touch with the subconscious than prior to your bout with daily reflection.

PROPER REFLECTION IS an art that many people misunderstand. The path to activating a successful EI is pursued along reflection habits that are consistent yet unstructured. To reflect in a way that is beneficial, it is best to explore your own strategies. However here are the steps that will let you find your own path and get you on your way.

THERE ARE many forms of reflection – each fine tuned to achieve a different end result. For the purpose of reaching EI, there is also a specific method of reflection that can be pursued. Remember there are many others you can probably do, but this one will get you to being emotionally intelligent in the shortest possible time.

THIS REFLECTION TECHNIQUE is designed to invoke your insight and your internal subconscious problem solving mechanisms to come to the forefront and vibrate at a frequency that is similar to your consciousness. While all these may make the process sound daunting, it is not. It is one of the simplest. You start with a breathing exercise.

THE BREATHING EXERCISE is meant to calm your senses and increase your state of awareness. The awareness you invoke here will slowly become a part of your personality. The breathing exercise is merely accomplished by watching your breath. Tune your entire being to just accomplishing one task whale you do this and that is to watch yourself breathe.

DO NOT ATTEMPT to control your breathing in any way. Let your breathing take its own course and allow it to happen naturally. As you do this you will become aware of your breath's cadence and rhythm and you will undoubtedly feel the affinity between your breath and the presence of the entire world. Continue to watch your breathing and introduce yourself to the concept of being mindful.

MINDFULNESS

Mindfulness is intricately woven into the concept of Emotional Intelligence. EI is the ensuing result of a mindful existence because Mindfulness aligns the resources of the mind to their rightful tasks. Just as the conscious mind is designed to handle lower number of data streams and the subconscious is designed to process much larger amounts, mindfulness aligns the conscious mind to pay attention to the present moment while the rest is relegated to the subconscious.

THE KEY THING TO take away from this is that there doesn't need to be a specific set of practices to invoke the state of mindfulness and thereabout bring on the benefits of being emotionally intelligent. The thing that gets the ball rolling is the fact that one starts with being mindful and allocates the conscious mind to the present moment and frees up the subconscious to handle everything else. When this is done accurately, the person no longer gets overwhelmed in situations that would otherwise present a significant challenge.

BEING mindful is a significant ally in the quest of attaining an emotionally intelligent life and enjoying the consequences of it. To be mindful one just needs to begin to realize the following steps and incorporate them into their daily lives.

STEP #1

Your first step in invoking mindfulness, and by extension, your first step in taking on a life that is inline with EI, is to focus on the present with your consciousness. In a world that promotes multitasking that seems counterintuitive. But if you really take moment to think about it, it's not. Being mindful is not the antithesis of being productive or multitasking. In fact it is a higher level of multitasking. How? Well, by assigning the conscious mind to present tasks and allowing your subconscious to handle the other tasks, the multitasking is promoted at full steam. You can now even contemplate while you sleep, because the subconscious never sleeps and it will be good to put it to work while you and your consciousness get some rest.

AS SUCH, your first step is to focus your mind into looking at the most important aspect of your existence, which is breathing. Watch your breath and let everything else fade into the background on its own. Do not force it. Just watch your breath and nothing else.

STEP #2

As you watch your breath, do not seek to control it, but rather measure each breath by the way you feel. Inhalation results in one feeling, while exhaling results in something else. Subtle as they may be, there is a difference. Keep watching for that difference.

STEP #3

You can do this exercise anywhere. On the train; on the bus, at home in your room. Where and when are not important because as time passes this will be your natural state. This is not prayer, nor meditation. Being mindful simple prepares your mind to take on different tasks. Begin to practice this once a day, then escalate the frequency to twice, then three time and take it to a point that you do it every time your watch indicates the top of the hour. Within a week of starting you will have got to the point that you will be spending a few moments of mindfulness at the top of every hour.

STEP #4

Once you get to the point you can invoke a state of mindfulness at the top of every hour, it's only a matter of practice that will result in you being mindful at every moment in time.

IT JUST TAKES you four steps to introduce the mind to being mindful and being resourceful in allocating the proper parts of the mind to the appropriate task. This is because the mind was built to do this and can get used to it very quickly if we give it a chance.

REFLECTION AND MINDFULNESS

Reflection and mindfulness go hand in hand in getting your mind and body to go into a state of being Emotionally Intelligent. If you recall being emotionally intelligent is about allowing greater amounts of data streams to be processed without getting overwhelmed or making the wrong conclusion.

ONCE YOU GET the step of being mindful, then the reflection sessions that you experience will be extremely beneficial. This is because while you remain mindful of the present, you will effectively 'record' whatever happens at that moment and your reflection times will be able to rely on accurate data, making your consciousness and subconsciousness have fewer inconsistencies.

.   .   .

THE MORE YOU PRACTICE MINDFULNESS, the better your reflection sessions will turnout. With better reflection sessions, you will be able to transfer data and analysis freely between your consciousness and subconsciousness thereby allowing yourself to be make better decisions.

THE POWER of reflection lies in its ability to strengthen one's mind. You will find that better reflection results in better analysis of a situation and with more practice, you will be able to make instantaneous analysis of complex situations. All this will not be done in your conscious mind but rather in your subconscious, although it may seem like it's in your conscious mind. The responses will be instantaneous.

19

Combining EQ with IQ

It would be negligent of this book to look at EQ solely without relating its benefits and powers to the IQ aspect of the mind. Relying on EQ alone has great effect for most people while relying on IQ alone is not as powerful. However there is one other option: to be able to develop both, EQ and IQ in tandem.

The holistic approach to mental clarity and mental superiority is enveloped in the ability to take advantage of both realms of the mind: EQ and IQ. Taking each on its own, results in a partial benefit. But when you take them together you start to see results. But since most people are IQ-heavy and EQ-deficient, most sources just make the case for enhancing the EQ portion of the person in the hopes that the IQ portion will continue and at some point the two will find a harmonious balance.

However, we do not plan to make that assumption. We will look at the way to ideally integrate the two that will result in a better life and a more successful existence.

Your first step is to look at which aspect you are more biased towards. Are you more EQ or are you more IQ centric. If you are more IQ, then this book will have the most impact for you. When you are constantly handling everything in your consciousness, it can get a little tiring and you will find that the lack of anything to do on the part of the subconscious also has its downside. An idle subconscious usually results in depression and lack of direction.

The first step to combining a powerful EQ with a developed IQ is to look at the state you currently experience. If you are more of Characteristic Q traits then Characteristic P traits, it is likely that your personality is more EQ centric – but that is not always the case as most people have a little bit of both. So the test will only get you to the point of giving you some insight but only upon proper reflection will you realize that you are more EQ or more IQ. I have found one simple test that you can subject yourself to if you want to understand which you are.

Assuming you cook, are you the kind of person that looks at recipes and measures every last ingredient down to its last ounce? Or, are you the kind of person that cooks from the seat of your pants. I find that this test is fairly accurate. You can substitute cooking for almost any other task. Just keep in mind that the art of not measuring your ingredients is not about precision but it means that the person is so in tune with the art, that they do not need external indicators to define the outcome. This is a classic example of a person governed by a higher EQ.

Once you understand that you are either dominated by EQ or IQ, you can then look at how to go about balancing your self. If you are IQ centric, start with the mindful exercise and look to reflection as a way of putting yourself on a path to developing your EQ side. The benefit of this is that you will be able to enhance yourself quickly. Any exercise to develop EQ is not an attempt to diminish your IQ side.

The EQ portion of your personality is always present and as you make a conscious effort to resurrect its dominance, you will find that it indeed comes easily. The human mind was designed with both aspects, but because of the importance that has been placed on one over the other, it is often mistakenly overlooked. It is not accurate to describe the human design as being only able to rely on IQ or only rely on EQ. We become who we chose to be, or rather the path that we are placed on by our caregivers and society at large.

Once you have developed the EQ side of the equation with mindfulness exercises, then it's time to integrate it with your IQ side. This is the simple part. To do this, you just need to follow three steps.

Step #1

Do not react to every situation before first subjecting the reaction to logic and reason. Logic and reason can be found on both sides of the mind – within the IQ side, logic and reason are a measurable step-by-step process that can be overseen. However, the logic and reason on the EQ side are instantaneous and are not easily monitored. The point is that you need to subject each response to a review by both sides. The correct response is usually something that you will have agreement from both sides.

Step #2

Enforce your reflection time to be accomplished on a daily basis. Although mindfulness is a constant state, reflection must be accomplished on a daily schedule so that the mind, both the EQ side and the IQ side can learn from experience. Learning from experience is a way to refine your time and actions in this world and become more in tune to the consequences of each action and to consequences of a series of actions. Most wrong moves are made because the person does not understand or can foresee the consequence of that move. Reflection changes that.

Step #3

Practice the act of having faith in your decisions. Every time you make a decision that is scrutinized by both sides, have faith in the outcome. Stop worrying about what may or may not happen. Faith is not about religion or spirituality in this case. Faith in this instance is about knowing that when you decide with both halves working for you, EQ and IQ, the decision that ensues is very likely the correct one. However, if you find the outcome unsatisfactory, you need to scrutinize if your expectations that is neither part of your EQ or IQ, but rather your imagination, that is faulty. Do not allow your imagination to create false expectations. False expectations will only result in you diminishing the power of a combined EQ and IQ.

With these three steps you are now on your way to realizing the benefits of a powerful EQ and IQ. You started with an understanding of what the EQ is and now you have learnt to develop it and finally you have seen how to combine it to your IQ to make your existence a formidable one.

Afterword

The one thing that we can take away from all this is that the mind is complex. Confining the concept of the mind to the physical function of the brain is usually the first problem. To be able to understand our potential as humans, start by stepping away from the concept of the brain. Look, instead, at the concept of the mind and the ability to connect that mind to the universe of nature around us.

The start of this journey is the differentiation of the EQ and the IQ. We can interchange the IQ to mean the cognitive version of the mind or we can look at it as the consciousness. It is the part we are usually aware of.

EQ has taken the world by storm, but looking at it in isolation is not an optimal course of action. It is powerful on its own but it is still limited if we do not take the power of EQ with the balance of the cognitive centers of the mind.

IQ, on its own, is a proposition that is worse of than EQ in many ways. IQ is limited in its application and it is unable to manage the voluminous amounts of data that sophisticated life comes attached with; while EQ is not capable of handling simple tasks effectively and in a timely fashion. Which is one of the reasons you find people with EQ-centric personalities bored with menial tasks and momentary situations. Sometimes they miss out on the simpler things in life because their IQ, or cognitive is just not in gear to take advantage of it.

To live a happy life, you need to be balanced. You need to take advantage of both EQ and IQ and in so doing live life to the fullest.

Bibliography

Goleman, D. (1998). *Working with Emotional Intelligence.*

Grayson, R. (n.d.). *Emotional Intelligence: A Summary.*

Kant, S., & Sharma, Y. (2012). A Study of Relationship Between Emotional Intelligence and Stress Among Teachers. *Technologia: A Journal of Science, Technology and Management,* 25-43.

Mayer, J. D. (1997). *What is Emotional Intelligence?* New York City : Basic Books.

Neisser, U. ,. (1996). Intelligence: Knowns and Unknowns. *American Psychologists,* 77-100.